THE PATHS OF LIFE

Reflections on the Readings for the Weekdays
of Advent and the Christmas Season

*Reflections on the Readings for the Weekdays
of Advent and the Christmas Season*

The Paths of Life

Ernest Ferlita, SJ

ALBA·HOUSE   NEW·YORK

SOCIETY OF ST. PAUL, 2187 VICTORY BLVD., STATEN ISLAND, NEW YORK 10314

ST PAULS

All scriptural quotations, except for one noted in the text, are from the New American Bible,© 1970 by the Confraternity of Christian Doctrine, including the Revised New Testament, © 1986. The one exception is from the New Revised Standard Version (NRSV).

Library of Congress Cataloging-in-Publication Data

Ferlita, Ernest.
    The paths of life: reflections on the readings for the weekdays of Advent and the Christmas season / Ernest Ferlita.
        p.   cm.
    Includes bibliographical references.
    ISBN: 0-8189-0828-9
    1. Advent Meditations.   2. Christmas Meditations.   3. Bible — Liturgical lessons, English Meditations.   4. Catholic Church Prayer-books and devotions — English.   I. Title.
    BX2170.A4F47   1999
    242'.33 — dc21   99-33224
                                                                    CIP

Published in the United States of America by the
Fathers and Brothers of the Society of St. Paul,
2187 Victory Boulevard, Staten Island, New York 10314-6603,
as part of their communications apostolate.

ISBN: 0-8189-0828-9

Printing Information:

Current Printing - first digit   1   2   3   4   5   6   7   8   9   10

Year of Current Printing - first year shown

1999   2000   2001   2002   2003   2004   2005   2006   2007   2008

CONTENTS

CHRISTMAS SEASON

FOREWORD

This is the fourth book that bears the title *The Paths of Life.*
That title comes from Peter's speech at Pentecost, when he
declares that God raised Jesus from the dead, as foretold by
David in the Greek translation of Psalm 16:

> You have made known to me the paths of life;
> you will fill me with joy in your presence (Ac 2:28).

Through word and action God makes known the paths of life.
I therefore call these reflections on God's words and actions *The
Paths of Life.*

Most of these reflections were given as homilies to the Poor
Clares in St. Clare's Monastery in New Orleans. A very recep-
tive, attentive, and encouraging assembly of listeners. I thank
them all.

Biblical Abbreviations

OLD TESTAMENT

Genesis	Gn	Nehemiah	Ne	Baruch	Ba
Exodus	Ex	Tobit	Tb	Ezekiel	Ezk
Leviticus	Lv	Judith	Jdt	Daniel	Dn
Numbers	Nb	Esther	Est	Hosea	Ho
Deuteronomy	Dt	1 Maccabees	1 M	Joel	Jl
Joshua	Jos	2 Maccabees	2 M	Amos	Am
Judges	Jg	Job	Jb	Obadiah	Ob
Ruth	Rt	Psalms	Ps	Jonah	Jon
1 Samuel	1 S	Proverbs	Pr	Micah	Mi
2 Samuel	2 S	Ecclesiastes	Ec	Nahum	Na
1 Kings	1 K	Song of Songs	Sg	Habakkuk	Hab
2 Kings	2 K	Wisdom	Ws	Zephaniah	Zp
1 Chronicles	1 Ch	Sirach	Si	Haggai	Hg
2 Chronicles	2 Ch	Isaiah	Is	Malachi	Ml
Ezra	Ezr	Jeremiah	Jr	Zechariah	Zc
		Lamentations	Lm		

NEW TESTAMENT

Matthew	Mt	Ephesians	Ep	Hebrews	Heb
Mark	Mk	Philippians	Ph	James	Jm
Luke	Lk	Colossians	Col	1 Peter	1 P
John	Jn	1 Thessalonians	1 Th	2 Peter	2 P
Acts	Ac	2 Thessalonians	2 Th	1 John	1 Jn
Romans	Rm	1 Timothy	1 Tm	2 John	2 Jn
1 Corinthians	1 Cor	2 Timothy	2 Tm	3 John	3 Jn
2 Corinthians	2 Cor	Titus	Tt	Jude	Jude
Galatians	Gal	Philemon	Phm	Revelation	Rv

THE PATHS OF LIFE

Reflections on the Readings for the Weekdays
of Advent and the Christmas Season

ADVENT

MONDAY OF THE FIRST WEEK OF ADVENT

Is 2:1-5;   Mt 8:5-11

A TIME OF WATCHING, WAITING, LONGING

Advent — a time of watching, waiting, longing,
which is aptly expressed in the opening prayer:
"Lord our God, help us to prepare
for the coming of the Lord.
May he find us waiting, eager in joyful prayer."

In the first reading, Isaiah,
one of the great prophets of Advent,
presents us with a vision indeed worth longing for —
a vision of universal peace,
a vision of God's kingdom to which all peoples,
Gentiles as well as Jews, shall come.
At its center is the mountain of the Lord's house,
towards which all nations shall stream.

Today's gospel is a bright reshaping of this vision.
The centurion, a Gentile, comes to Christ.
Yes, Christ is now the center, to whom all must come.
This tells us something more about Advent.
Our longing is filled with, or fueled with, faith —
faith in the power of Jesus, in the power of his word.
The centurion had that faith:
"Amen, I say to you, in no one in Israel
have I found such faith" (8:10).

There are two things to note:
first, faith calls forth Jesus' power,
the faith of the centurion calls forth power,

not for himself but for his servant.
And secondly, the centurion says that Jesus
doesn't have to go to his servant;
all he has to do is just say the word,
and the servant, though distant in space, will be healed.
So now we, distant in time,
will experience Christ's healing
if, like the centurion, we come to him with faith.

At communion, echoing the centurion,
we will say in the spirit of Advent:
"Lord, I am not worthy to receive you,
but only say the word and I shall be healed."

TUESDAY OF THE FIRST WEEK OF ADVENT
Is 11:1-10; Lk 10:21-24

EYES THAT SEE, EARS THAT HEAR

"Blessed are the eyes that see what you see" (Lk 10:23).
Jesus is talking to the seventy-two disciples
whom he had sent out in pairs
to all the towns and places
that he himself was to visit.
And what is it they see?
They see Jesus.
"For I say to you, many prophets and kings
desired to see what you see, but did not see it,
and to hear what you hear, but did not hear it" (10:24).

In the first reading the prophet Isaiah
describes with great power

the vision of him who is to come.
"[A] shoot shall sprout from the stump of Jesse" (Is 11:1).
Jesse was the father of King David,
and the messianic king would blossom
like a bud from the roots of David's dynasty.
"The spirit of the Lord shall rest upon him:
a spirit of wisdom and understanding,
a spirit of counsel and strength,
a spirit of knowledge and fear of the Lord" (11:2).
And peace and justice and reconciliation
will flourish in his kingdom.
"The calf and the young lion shall browse together,
with a little child to guide them" (11:6).

Jesus is that little child,
and that little child is the messianic king.
"All things have been handed over to me by my Father.
No one knows who the Son is except the Father
and who the Father is except the Son and anyone
to whom the Son wishes to reveal him" (Lk 11:22).
And to whom does the Son wish to reveal him?
To the merest children, to the "childlike" (11:21),
not to the learned and the clever,
not to those whose pride prevents them
from seeing into the depths of reality.

God help us, in this time of Advent;
God bless our eyes and ears
that we may see and hear him who is to come.

WEDNESDAY OF THE FIRST WEEK OF ADVENT
Is 25:6-10;   Mt 15:29-37

A GREAT FORESHADOWING

Both readings situate us on a mountain,
and we are in the midst of a great crowd of people.
In Isaiah the mountain is Mount Zion,
a symbol of the new Jerusalem,
where all peoples, not just the people of Israel,
gather for the messianic banquet.

In the gospel a large number of people
follow Jesus up the mountain.
Are they only the people of Israel?
Certainly most of them are.
But it's worth noting that, right before this episode,
Jesus encountered the Canaanite woman
who begged him to heal her daughter.
At first he said not a word in answer to her;
but then he said he had been sent
"only to the lost sheep of the house of Israel."
But the woman kept pleading for his help,
and finally he gave in, saying,
"O woman, great is your faith!
Let it be done for you as you wish" (Mt 15:22-28).
And her daughter was healed.

The people who came to him on the mountain
brought friends and relatives to be healed,
"the lame, the blind, the deformed,
the mute, and many others" (15:30).
Healings *now* are a sign of healings *forever*.

"Behold,... I perform healings today and tomorrow,
and on the third day
I accomplish my purpose" (Lk 13:32).

In Isaiah, too, the Lord God will do likewise.
"On this mountain [the Lord God] will destroy
the veil that veils all peoples...
he will destroy death forever.
The Lord God will wipe away the tears
from all faces" (Is 25:8-9).

And in both readings there is a great foreshadowing
of the Eucharist, the bread of everlasting life.
"On this mountain," says Isaiah, "the Lord of hosts
will provide for all peoples,
a feast of rich food and choice wines" (25:1-2).
In the gospel Jesus says of the people,
"I do not wish to send them away hungry,
for fear they may collapse on the way" (Mt 15:32).
There follows immediately
the multiplication of the loaves and fishes.
Jesus "took the seven loaves and the fish,
gave thanks, broke the loaves,
and gave them to the disciples,
who in turn gave them to the crowds" (15:36).

With this in mind, we pray again the opening prayer:
"Lord our God, grant that we may be ready
to receive Christ when he comes in glory
and to share in the banquet of heaven."

THURSDAY OF THE FIRST WEEK OF ADVENT
Is 26:1-6;   Mt 7:21, 24-27

THE GRACE TO KNOW GOD'S WILL

"Not everyone who says to me, Lord, Lord,
will enter the kingdom of heaven,
but only the one who does the will
of my Father in heaven" (Mt 7:21).
The split that Jesus has reference to
is between saying and doing,
and he picks up on this idea in the parable that follows.
Here the split is between hearing and doing:
"Everyone who listens to these words of mine
and acts on them will be like a wise man
who built his house on rock" (7:23).
It will not collapse in the winds and rain of a hurricane.
"And everyone who listens to these words of mine
but does not act on them will be like a fool
who built his house on sand" (7:26).
A house built on sand will collapse.
This parable concludes the Sermon on the Mount.
When Jesus says "listens to these words of mine"
he has reference to everything he has just said.

The wise disciple acts decisively
by building his whole life
on the rock foundation of Jesus' words.
He's like the strong city Isaiah describes:
"Trust in the Lord forever!" he says,
"For the Lord is an eternal rock" (Is 26:4).
"The wise disciple realizes
that these words of Jesus the Son

are identical with 'the will of my Father.'
Consequently the wise disciple forms his whole existence
according to these words; he *does* them."[1]

The words of Jesus represent God's general will for us all.
We can also speak of God's particular will for each of us.
It's a very particular will indeed for Jesus,
when he says in the agony of the garden:
"Not my will, but yours be done."
To find God's particular will for me:
that's what the Spiritual Exercises is all about.
From the very beginning St. Ignatius urges the exercitant
"to ask God for what I want and desire" (no. 48).
And the hope is that by the end of the Exercises
what I want and desire will be God's will for me.
Ignatius would almost always end his letters with this wish
(and we'll end these reflections with it):
"May God give you abundant grace to know his will
and fulfill it perfectly."

FRIDAY OF THE FIRST WEEK OF ADVENT
Is 29:17-24;   Mt 9:27-31

SPIRITUAL BLINDNESS

A Canadian priest by the name of Emiliano Tardiff
once held a healing service for some 4,000 people
on the Ivory Coast, and the next day
one of the priests who had been there said to him:

---

[1] John P. Meier, *Matthew*, 75.

"Father, last night you did something
that was contrary to the Gospel.
When Jesus healed the sick,
he forbade them to speak about the miracle,
while last night you asked those who had been healed
to proclaim it to the world."
Father Tardiff replied:
"At the beginning of his public life, Jesus did not want
to reveal his messianic identity too abruptly,
and that is why he used to say, 'Don't tell it to anyone.'
But on the day of his ascension, he ordered
that we proclaim the gospel to the ends of the earth."[2]

Yes, oddly enough, we find Jesus *sternly* warning
the two blind men he had healed not to tell anyone.
But they did.
They went off and spread the word of him
in the whole area. I said "oddly enough"
because in the episode just before this
Jesus had raised an official's daughter from the dead
and news of this quickly spread through all the land.
And in the episode following this one
he drives the demon out of a demoniac who was mute
and the crowds are amazed.
But the Pharisees say:
"He drives out demons by the prince of demons" (9:32).

Apparently that's one reason why he tried to control
the spreading of the word about what he did.
There were those like the Pharisees
whose pride in their own authority
made them spiritually blind.

---

[2] Emiliano Tardiff, *Jesus Is the Messiah*, 48-49.

To the two blind men before he touched their eyes
Jesus said, "Do you believe that I can do this?"
"Yes, Lord," they said.
They were not spiritually blind.
"Let it be done to you," Jesus said,
"according to your faith."
According to their faith.
It is because of their faith in Jesus' power to heal
that their eyes are opened.

Jesus is the fulfillment of Isaiah's messianic vision.
"…out of gloom and darkness
the eyes of the blind shall see.
The lowly will ever find joy in the Lord,
and the poor rejoice in the Holy One of Israel" (29:19).

Pray God that *we* may see.
May Jesus remove from us every spiritual blindness.
Let it be done to us according to our faith.
It is because of our faith in Jesus' power to heal
that our eyes are opened.
The Lord is our light and our salvation.
May we gaze on the loveliness of the Lord
all the days of our life.

SATURDAY OF THE FIRST WEEK OF ADVENT
Is 30:19-21, 23-26;   Mt 9:35-10:1, 6-8

GIVE FREELY WHAT YOU HAVE FREELY RECEIVED

Jesus summons his twelve apostles
and sends them to the lost sheep of Israel —

not to the Samaritans, not to the pagans,
but only to the lost sheep of the house of Israel.
It's as if he is doing now what we heard Isaiah say
that the Lord God would do for Israel:
"The Lord will give you the bread you need
and the water for which you thirst" (Is 30:20).
He will bind up their wounds and heal their bruises (v. 26).
This is the mission of the twelve apostles,
restricted for now to the people of Israel.
It is not until the end of Matthew's gospel
that their mission becomes universal.
"Go, therefore, and make disciples of all nations" (28:19).

And they are to do then what Jesus urged them to do
from the very beginning: they are to give freely
what they have freely received (Mt 10:8).
What Jesus said to his apostles, he says to us:
Give freely what you have freely received.

There's a corollary that flows from that principle.
In the world of spirit, there's *more* spirit
when you give it away, not less spirit.
Not so in the world of matter:
If I give something away, I don't have it anymore.
But in the world of spirit
giving spirit away causes it to multiply.
When I give my love to someone,
I don't have less love, I have more love.[3]

As we prayed in the opening prayer,
God so loved the world that he gave us his only Son.
Out of love for us Jesus gave his life

---

[3] Cf. John Shea, *Gospel Spirituality: An Audio Retreat*.

and was raised to new life.
Now in the Eucharist we give thanks to God;
we give thanks for the Christ
who reconciled us by his death
and saved us by his life.

MONDAY OF THE SECOND WEEK OF ADVENT
Is 35:1-10;   Lk 5:17-26

THE GREAT AMEN

The power of the Lord is with Jesus, we're told,
the power to heal.
There he is, teaching,
surrounded by a large crowd of people,
including a goodly number of scribes and Pharisees,
when some men who couldn't get through the crowd
climb to the roof of the house
and lower a paralyzed man through an opening
onto the floor in front of Jesus.
When Jesus sees their faith,
he says to the paralyzed man,
"Your sins are forgiven" (Lk 5:20).
Now that is certainly something worth noting.
It's not that Jesus sees *his* faith,
he sees *their* faith.
Faith, yes, draws power out from him,
but it's not the faith of the one in need,
but the faith of his friends.
They form a community of faith.
Then and now, healing comes from God
through the community.

Then and now, Jesus speaks in God's name
and in the name of the community:
"Your sins are forgiven."

But there are those present
who did not share this faith,
the scribes and the Pharisees,
and they began to ask themselves,
"Who is this who speaks blasphemies?
Who but God alone can forgive sins?" (5:21).
And Jesus, sensing their thoughts, says in reply:
"Which is easier — to say,
'Your sins are forgiven,'
or to say, 'Rise and walk'?" (5:23).

Gerard Manley Hopkins comments on these words.
Jesus doesn't "say 'Which is easier to *do?*'
for we know it is easier to heal the body than the soul.
But the question is: 'Which is easier to *say?*'
Which costs the speaker most?
…any imposter can say, ['Your sins are forgiven'].
Who will know? The soul is not seen…
But say to a cripple, 'Arise and walk,'
and the next minute you have power from God or no."[4]
So then Jesus says to the scribes and Pharisees,
"But that you may know that the Son of Man
has authority on earth to forgive sins" —
he says to the paralytic, "I say to you,
rise, pick up your stretcher, and go home" (5:24).
And the man is healed, he is freed.
As we heard Isaiah say in the first reading,
dreaming of his people's freedom:

---

[4] *Sermons and Writings*, 28.

"The lame shall leap like a stag!"
And astonishment seized everybody who saw it
and "struck with awe," they cried out,
"We have seen incredible things today" (5:26).

Jesus embodies the Father's authority to forgive sins,
embodies his power to heal, his will to heal.
"This is what the Father wants," Jesus says, in effect,
"your health and salvation.
Such is his gracious will."
To that will I say Yes, to that will I say Amen.
Jesus not only says yes, he *is* yes;
he not only says Amen, he *is* Amen.
Jesus is the great "Amen,
the faithful and true witness" (Rv 3:14).

TUESDAY OF THE SECOND WEEK OF ADVENT
Is 40:1-11; Mt 18:12-14

AN IMAGE OF CHRIST

Today in the first reading from Isaiah
we hear again the great cry of Advent:
Prepare the way of the Lord!
Make straight... a highway for our God!
The Lord God comes to save,
he comes with power to rule with a strong arm.
This same Lord is seen as the good shepherd,
who "feeds his flock"
and "gathers the lambs" in his arms,
"carrying them in his bosom,
and leading the ewes with care" (40:11).

In the gospel Jesus recreates this image
of the Good Shepherd in a very striking way.
"If a man has a hundred sheep
and one of them goes astray,
will he not leave the ninety-nine in the hills
and go in search of the stray?
And if he finds it, amen, I say to you,
he rejoices more over it
than over the ninety-nine that did not stray" (18:12-13).

For the early Christians
this was a favorite image of Christ.
In the Priscilla catacombs in Rome there is a fresco
depicting Christ as the Good Shepherd:
He is seen as a young man
dressed in a tunic fastened at the left shoulder,
and he carries a sheep slung over his shoulders.
Why does he carry it?
Because it is weak, or injured perhaps, or ill.
To carry the sheep is to care for it.
It is a sign of Christ's love and mercy,
much like the sacrament of anointing.

WEDNESDAY OF THE SECOND WEEK OF ADVENT
Is 40:25-31;   Mt 11:28-30

TRUST IN THE LORD

"Can we trust in the Lord?"
That question is implicit in both readings.
In the first reading, God addresses the Israelites

who are returning from the Babylonian captivity.
Can they trust in the Lord?
"Do you not know," he says,
"or have you not heard?
The Lord is the eternal God,
creator of the ends of the earth...
They that hope in the Lord will renew their strength,
they will soar as with eagles' wings" (40:28, 31).

In the gospel, too, what Jesus says
can be heard as an answer to the question:
Can we trust in the Lord?
"Come to me, all you who labor and are burdened,
and I will give you rest."
Jesus reaches out to help us.
"Take my yoke upon you," he says.
"For my yoke is easy, and my burden light" (11:28-30).

Legend has it that Jesus the carpenter
was the best yokemaker in Galilee:
his yokes were always fitted to the ox
so as not to gall its neck. (In today's jargon,
as someone suggested, they were "user-friendly.")
And quite possibly when Jesus says,
"Take my yoke upon you,"
he's talking about a double yoke,
a yoke that was borne by two oxen.
And that's why the burden of his yoke is "light":
Jesus is right there beside me and he bears it with me.

Can we trust in Lord?
I trust, Lord; help thou my lack of trust.

THURSDAY OF THE SECOND WEEK OF ADVENT
Is 41:13-20;   Mt 11:11-15

THE GREATEST IN THE KINGDOM OF HEAVEN

From today until the end of Advent
John the Baptist is mentioned,
even featured, in the Gospel readings.
And Jesus in today's gospel indicates why:
"...among those born of women
there has been none greater than John the Baptist."
He surpasses all the prophets that came before him.
He brings to its climax everything they prophesied,
and he announces the embodiment, in Jesus,
of the kingdom of God.
And "if you are willing to accept it," Jesus tells the people,
"he is Elijah, the one who is to come."
But not all were, or are, willing to accept it.
Orthodox Jews, I'm told, still place an empty chair
for Elijah at each yearly Seder meal.
"They do so, hoping this will be the year Elijah will return
to prepare the way for the Messiah's coming."[5]

There is none greater than John the Baptist
precisely for this reason:
he prepared the way of the Lord.
And yet, Jesus says, "the least in the kingdom of heaven
is greater than he" (Mt 11:11).
John, great as he is, belongs to the Old Order;
the least in the kingdom belongs to the New.

---

[5] Mark Link, S.J., *Advent/Christmas 2000, Year C*, 22.

Who is the least?
Any of Jesus' disciples, any of his "little ones."
Later, Jesus' disciples will ask him,
"Who is the greatest in the kingdom of heaven?"
Jesus calls a child over and places it in their midst.
"Whoever humbles himself like this child
is the greatest in the kingdom of heaven" (18:4).

But even the greatest are subject to persecution.
"From the days of John the Baptist until now,"
Jesus says, "The kingdom of heaven suffers violence,
and the violent are taking it by force" (11:12).
A difficult saying, and Matthew may well be talking
more about his own time than the time of Jesus,
but the sense of what he's saying would seem to be
that the violent opponents of the kingdom
do all they can to snatch it away from those who want it.[6]
Let those who want it take to heart the words
that the Lord speaks to the captive people of Israel,
as we heard in the first reading from Isaiah:
"I am the Lord, your God, who grasp your right hand;
It is I who say to you, 'Fear not, I will help you'" (41:13).

With these thoughts we *pray* again the opening prayer:
"Almighty Father, give us the joy of your love
to prepare the way for Christ our Lord.
Help us to serve you and one another."
To serve, not to be served:
whoever humbles himself, like Christ,
is the greatest in the kingdom of heaven.

---

[6] Cf. John P. Meier, *Matthew*, 122.

FRIDAY OF THE SECOND WEEK OF ADVENT
Is 48:17-19;   Mt 11:16-19

GOD'S WISDOM

In the opening prayer we prayed:
"May we live as he (our Savior) has taught."
And in the closing prayer we will pray:
"Teach us, [Father], to live by your wisdom."

If people criticized both John and Jesus,
as we heard in the gospel,
more than likely it was basically for the same reason:
Jesus seemed to put himself above the law,
and John, after all, pointed to Jesus
as the one who is to come,
the one whom, according to Matthew,
"[a]ll the prophets and the law prophesied" (11:13).

The law, the Torah, was God's wisdom,
the source of revelation and salvation.
As we heard Isaiah say,
"If you would hearken to my commandments,
your prosperity would be like a river,
and your vindication like the waves of the sea" (48:18).
And in the responsorial psalm: "Happy the one
who... delights in the law of the Lord" (1:1, 2).

As Jesus said to the people,
"Do not think that I have come
to abolish the law and the prophets.
I have come not to abolish but to fulfill" (Mt 5:17),
to fulfill its purpose of revelation and salvation.

He is the true knowledge communicated by God,
he is the key to union with God,
he is God's wisdom incarnate.
"[W]isdom is vindicated by her works,"
as we heard him say in the gospel (11:19).

Which prompts us to end as we began:
"May we live as he (our Savior) has taught."
"Teach us, [Father], to live by your wisdom."

SATURDAY OF THE SECOND WEEK OF ADVENT
Si 48:1-4, 9-11;   Mt 17:10-13

THE DAYBREAK FROM ON HIGH

"Chariots of fire" is a phrase made familiar to us
by a film with that title about the runner Eric Liddell.
As we heard in the first reading,
it's a reference to the prophet Elijah
taken up to heaven in a fiery chariot (Si 48:9).
This led to a persistent and pervasive belief:
that Elijah would return "to put an end to wrath
before the day of the Lord," to "turn back
the hearts of fathers toward their [children]" (48:10),
and "the hearts of children to their fathers" (Ml 3:24).

It is Elijah who appears with Moses
at Jesus' transfiguration on a high mountain,
and the question that the disciples put to Jesus
in today's gospel occurs as they come down the mountain.
"Why do the scribes say that Elijah must come first?"

In the beginning of his answer,
Jesus seems to identify Elijah with himself:
"Elijah will indeed come and will restore all things."
But then he says, "Elijah has already come,"
meaning John the Baptist,
"and they did not recognize him
and did to him whatever they pleased.
So also," he says, referring to himself again,
"will the Son of Man suffer at their hands" (17:10-12).
The disciples understood, but only about John the Baptist;
they did not understand that Jesus had to suffer and die.

But just as the divinity of Jesus, at the Transfiguration,
shone in the radiance of his flesh,
so at his birth the "daybreak from on high"
breaks into our world (Lk 2:78).
The Father says at both events: "This is my Beloved Son."

As we prayed in the opening prayer:
"Lord, let your glory dawn to take away our darkness.
May we be revealed as the children of light
at the coming of your Son."

MONDAY OF THE THIRD WEEK OF ADVENT
Nb 24:2-7, 15-17;   Mt 21:23-27

THE STAR OF JACOB

One of the earliest known paintings
of the Madonna and Child dates back to the 2nd century.
It's on the wall in the catacombs of Priscilla in Rome.

The painting is not too well preserved.
But still visible is the prophet Balaam,
standing near the Madonna
and pointing to the star of Jacob above her head.
Even though the evangelists never mention this prophecy,
the painting shows how from the earliest church
it was seen as fulfilled in Christ:
"A star shall advance from Jacob,
and a staff shall rise from Israel" (Nb 24:17).

It was, in a sense, the answer to the question
that the Pharisees in today's gospel put to Jesus:
"By what authority are you doing these things?
And who gave you this authority?" (21:23).
"These things" that they are asking about
are things that Matthew has just described:
his triumphal entry into Jerusalem,
the driving out of the temple area
"all those engaged in selling and buying there,"
healing the blind and the lame who come to him,
allowing children to cry out to him,
"Hosanna to the son of David" (21:1-15).

When asked a question of this sort,
Jesus counters with a question of his own.
"If you answer it for me, then I shall tell you
by what authority I do these things.
What was the origin of John's baptism?
Was it divine or merely human?" (21:24-25).
Jesus is not being evasive.
"He is trying to get his interrogators
to look beyond appearances,
to search their own hearts"
for reasons why they judge as they do.

He requires this of us too —
"not only when it is a matter
of observing the actions of others
but even more when it comes
to discerning his action in our own lives."
Our task is to see, "to understand."[7]

Pray for light,
that the eye of our eyes may be opened,
that we may recognize Christ in others,
that we may see him more clearly,
love him more ardently,
and follow him more closely.

TUESDAY OF THE THIRD WEEK OF ADVENT
Zp 3:1-2, 9-13;   Mt 21:28-32

SPEECH AND ACTION

One of Matthew's favorite themes is "the split
in the religious person between saying and doing."[8]
Saying and doing, speech and action:
that's one way of describing the theme of today's readings.
In Zephaniah we read:
"I will change and purify the lips of the peoples" (3:9)
or as another translation has it,
"I will change the speech of the peoples
to a pure speech." (NRSV)

---

[7]   Brian Moore, S.J., *The Gospel Day by Day through Advent*, 56.

[8]   John P. Meier, *Matthew*, 240.

To what effect?
"That all may call on the name of the Lord
[*and*] serve him with one accord."
Speech *and* action: both working in accord.
"They shall do no wrong and speak no lies;
nor shall there be found in their mouths
a deceitful tongue" (3:13).
As Jesus said:
"It is not those who say to me, 'Lord, Lord,'
who will enter the kingdom of heaven,
but the person who does the will of the Father" (Mt 7:21).

"What is your opinion?" (3:28).
Jesus, in today's gospel, asks this
of the chief priests and elders of the people.
And he tells them the parable of the two sons.
When the father asks the first son
to go work in the vineyard, he answers, "No, I will not,"
but afterwards he changes his mind and goes.
Speech at first refuses action,
but then action reverses speech
so that speech and action are now in accord.

The second son says, "Yes, sir," but then he doesn't go.
Speech and action are in contradiction, like those who say,
"Lord, Lord," but do not do his will.

When Jesus asks the chief priests and elders
which of the two sons did the will of the father,
they, of course, answered that it was the first,
the one who said no but then repented.
"Well then," Jesus says, "the tax-collectors and prostitutes
will enter the kingdom of heaven before you."
Why? Because by their action they had in effect said,

"I will not obey,"
but then when John came to show them the way
they repented. They had a change of heart, and believed.

On the other hand, the chief priests and elders,
like the second son, say, in effect, "I will obey,"
but it's only lip-service.
They pride themselves on how they obey the law of Moses,
but their interpretation of the law is so rigid
that they oppress the people by it.
When John comes to show them the way to righteousness,
they do not repent. There is no change of heart.
They remain fixed in their self-righteousness.
For them, speech and action are in contradiction,
like those who say, "Lord, Lord," but do not do his will.

Well, may speech and action be in accord for us.
We can imagine a third son not mentioned in the parable.
When this son is asked to go work in the vineyard,
he says, "Yes, sir," and indeed he does go.
This son is like Jesus himself, who says,
"Here I am, Lord," and does the will of the Father.
Let that mind which was in Christ Jesus be also in us.

WEDNESDAY OF THE THIRD WEEK OF ADVENT
Is 45:6-8, 18, 21-25;   Lk 7:18-23

THE FIRST COMING

"Let justice descend, O heavens, like dew from above,
like gentle rain let the skies drop it down.

Let the earth open and salvation bud forth,
let justice spring up" (Is 45:8).
The first half of this text used to be sung in Latin,
"Rorate coeli," to a haunting melody
that stirred up in me the spirit of Advent.

Advent invites us to a vivid remembrance of the past,
to a remembrance of Christ's first coming.
As John's disciples questioned Jesus,
"Are you the one who is to come,
or should we look for another?" (Lk 7:19),
Jesus answers in words that fulfill
more than one of Isaiah's prophecies:
"Go and tell John what you see and hear:
the blind regain their sight,
the lame walk, lepers are cleansed,
the deaf hear, the dead are raised,
the poor have the good news proclaimed to them" (7:22).

If our mind's eye is drawn to remembrance of the past,
what becomes of our attention to the present?
Actually, that attention is what Advent is all about.
By ritualizing Christ's first coming,
we experience what the people of old experienced,
their longing for salvation,
their yearning for the light,
and *through* that experiencing
we open the present to yet another coming of the Lord:
his coming into our lives here and now
through faith and hope and love,
as Paul proclaims in a prayer (Eph 3:18-19):
May Christ "dwell in your hearts through faith;
that you, rooted and grounded in love,
may have the strength

to comprehend with all the holy ones
what is the breadth and length and height and depth,
and to know the love of Christ that surpasses knowledge,
so that you may be filled with all the fullness of God."[9]

THURSDAY OF THE THIRD WEEK OF ADVENT
Is 54:1-10;   Lk 7:24-30

THE GREATEST AND THE LEAST

Who is the greatest? That's quite a question.
The greatest what? The greatest president?
The greatest writer, singer, athlete?
For each of those questions
we could come up with some answer.
But who is the greatest human being that ever lived?
How answer that?
The greatest, say, up to the time of Jesus.
That restricts it somewhat,
but it's still quite a question.

Jesus comes up with this answer:
"[A]mong those born of women,
no one is greater than John [the Baptist]" (7:28).
How are we to understand that?
No one is greater than John
because he ushers in the new age,
he prepares the way of the Lord,

---

[9] Adapted from *The Paths of Life, Cycle A*, 12-13.

which is like saying to the people,
"Your exile is over,
your redeemer has come to set you free."

As we heard Isaiah say to the people in exile:
"Your redeemer is the Holy One of Israel,
called God of all the earth.
The Lord calls you back,
like a wife forsaken and grieved in spirit,
[a] wife married in youth and then cast off,
says your God" (54:5-6).

No one is greater than John. And yet,
as we heard Jesus say in today's gospel
(as we heard him say in last Thursday's gospel),
"the least in the kingdom of heaven
is greater than he" (Lk 7:28).
John, great as he is, belongs to the Old Order;
the least in the kingdom belongs to the New.
Who is the least?
Any of Jesus' disciples, any of his "little ones."
Later, Jesus's disciples will ask him,
"Who is the greatest in the kingdom of Heaven?"
Jesus calls a child over and places it in their midst.
"Whoever humbles himself like this child
is the greatest in the kingdom of heaven" (18:4).

Prepare the way of the Lord.
Come, Lord Jesus.

FRIDAY OF THE THIRD WEEK OF ADVENT
Is 56:1-3, 6-8;   Jn 5:33-36

PRECONCEPTIONS

Captain Ronald Evans, a former astronaut,
once spoke about his adventure in space.
"When you're up there," he said,
"you can make whatever you see
agree with any previous conceptions
you may have about life.
The experience can't help but strengthen
any belief in whatever God you've had before.
You see the earth rotating,
see day go into night
and there are no strings attached."
"Previous conceptions" or, in a word, preconceptions.
Some years earlier a Soviet cosmonaut
said of his experience: "There is no god in the heavens."

Jesus knew all about preconceptions.
He said to the Pharisees: "You search the scriptures,
because you think you have eternal life through them;
even they testify on my behalf."
And yet, he says,
you refuse "to come to me to have life" (Jn 5:39-40).
These preconceptions prevent them
from seeing him for what he is.
But don't think "that I will accuse you," he says;
"the one who will accuse you is Moses,
in whom you have placed your hope.
For if you had believed Moses,
you would have believed me,

because he wrote about me" (5:45-46).
Moses accuses them as he accused the people of old
who begged Aaron to make for them
a god that will go before them (Ex 32:1);
he accuses them because their preconceptions,
like golden calves, go like gods before them,
blinding them to the true God revealed in Jesus.

Jesus appealed to his works.
As we heard him say,
"The works that the Father gave me to accomplish,
these works that I perform testify on my behalf
that the Father has sent me" (Jn 5:36).
For these works manifest his glory,
as did his first work at the wedding of Cana;
the same glory manifest from the beginning of time
in the work of creation:
"The heavens are telling the glory of God;
and the firmament proclaims his handiwork.
Day to day pours forth speech,
and night to night declares knowledge" (Ps 19:1-2).

The astronaut saw; the cosmonaut did not.
We too search the heavens;
we too search the scriptures.
Do we see the glory of God?
Or are we blinded by our golden calves?
What god goes before us?[10]

---

[10] Adapted from *Gospel Journey*, 71-72.

DECEMBER 17th
Gn 49:2, 8-10;   Mt 1:1-17

THE FAMILY TREE

The family tree branches out in all directions.
A lot of people, especially Americans,
try to trace their genealogies as far back as possible,
reaching into those countries
from which their parents or ancestors came.
Matthew's genealogy of Jesus
stresses his descent from Abraham,
in whose offspring "all the nations of the earth
shall find blessing" (Gn 22:18),
and from David, "king of the house of Judah" (1 S 2:4).

"By reciting Jesus' genealogy," we join Matthew
"in acknowledging Jesus' Jewishness,
which for Christians must be something more
than a mere historical fact from the past."
According to theologian Gerald O'Collins,
"all Christians should esteem and cherish
Jewish men and women as being in quite a special way
the brothers and sisters of Jesus."[11]

It's worth noting how special it was for some.
St. Edith Stein, shortly before her martyrdom,
said to her confessor:
"You don't know what it means to me
to be a daughter of the chosen people —

---

[11] Gerald O'Collins, S.J., *All Things New*, 16-17.

to belong to Christ, not only spiritually,
but according to the flesh."[12]
And on more than one occasion St. Ignatius Loyola
expressed the wish to be of the same blood as Christ.

But remarkably it's not "the blood in our veins
but the word of God in our hearts"
that relates us to Jesus,
that makes us members of the Lord's family.

"My mother and my brothers," he says,
"are those who hear the word of God
and act on it" (Lk 8:21).
The word of God that "we read and hear each day
is our link with the Lord."
But the link will not bind
unless we put God's word into practice.[13]

The word of God creates the family of God.
If we hear God's word and act on it,
we're happily related to one another,
through Jesus Christ, the Word made flesh.

---

[12] Waltraud Herbstrith, *Edith Stein*, 63.

[13] *Loose-Leaf Lectionary for Mass*, September 22, 1998, 3635.

DECEMBER 18th
Jr 23:5-8;   Mt 1:18-24

GOD SAVES

When Mary is found to be with child,
Joseph decides to break his engagement to her.
But he doesn't tell her right away.
He goes to bed thinking he'll tell her in the morning.
But while he is still sleeping,
he gets a divine message in a dream:
"Joseph, son of David," don't you know Mary?
Don't you know that her virtue is such
that she could not possibly have been unfaithful to you?
"It is by the Holy Spirit that she has conceived this child.
She is to have a son and you are to name him Jesus
because he will save his people from their sins" (1:21).

Yes, the very name of Jesus means "God saves."
He comes to save God's people, the great liberator
whose coming was predicted by all the prophets,
including Jeremiah who prophesies in today's first reading
that the Lord will "raise up a righteous shoot to David,"
who will "reign and govern wisely"
and "do what is just and right in the land" (23:5).
But it will not be a national liberation,
as most of Israel expected, but a spiritual liberation.[14]

Joseph, son of David, an upright man,
does as he is commanded to do.
He takes Mary as his wife and names her son Jesus.

---

[14] Cf. Meier, *Matthew*, 7-8.

Jesus, the power and mercy of God.

"In both the Old and New Testaments
the mercy of God meant, first of all,
his will to save before any act of ours.
God's mercy is the other side of his power.
The Ark of the Covenant
represented the seat of God's power.
The Ark is also known as the Mercy Seat.
Jesus is the Ark of the New Covenant.

In Jesus we become what, of ourselves,
we have no power to be.
Jesus will push the boundaries of human existence
as far as they can go.
He will expand the horizons of our being
beyond the furthest reach of our imaginations.
In Jesus the power of God is revealed, and the mercy.

That is why his name is above every other name."[15]

DECEMBER 19th
Jg 13:2-7, 24-25;   Lk 1:5-25

WHAT'S IN A NAME?

The angel Gabriel says to Zechariah:
"Your prayer has been heard."
What was Zechariah praying for? A son?

---

[15] Ferlita, *Gospel Journey*, 10-11.

Maybe so, even though he and his wife
were advanced in years.
When his wife Elizabeth conceives, she says:
"[T]he Lord... has seen fit
to take away my disgrace before others" (1:25).

Or maybe Zechariah was praying for the people —
we're told the people themselves were praying outside —
maybe he was praying for someone who,
to quote the angel Gabriel,
will turn many of the people
"to the Lord their God" (1:16).

The son that will be born to Elizabeth and Zechariah
is to be called John.
What's in a name, that the angel Gabriel
should declare what it will be?
Well, in ancient times a name often signified
a person's vocation, what he or she was called to be.
The name John, you may recall, means
"Yahweh is gracious";
Yehohannan, "Yahweh has shown his favor."

This is what John will proclaim
by the life he is destined to lead.
John is consecrated from his very conception
to the Lord's service.
Like Samson, as we heard in the first reading,
he is to live under the nazirite vow,
never drinking strong drink and eating nothing unclean.
Nazirite comes from the word *nazir*,
meaning "one set apart."
Like Samson, he is to be a sign to the people
of God's care and concern.

And they, in turn, are moved
to show care and concern for others.
And so should we be,
all the more when we look to him
for whom John prepares the way.

As we prayed in the third "O Antiphon,"
"Come, Flower of Jesse's stem,
sign of God's love for all his people:
save us without delay!"

DECEMBER 20th
Is 7:10-14;   Lk 1:26-38

CONSENT ILLUMINES MARY

Thomas Merton, the Trappist monk who wrote so well
about so many things, once said of the Virgin Mary:
she "did not obscure God's light in her being"
and therefore she is "in the highest sense a person."[16]
In Merton's mind, to be in the highest sense a person
meant not obscuring God's light in our being,
and that's what Mary can teach us.

How did Mary live so as not to obscure
God's light in her being?
A poet answers that question with these words:
"Consent illumines her."[17]

---

[16] Quoted in John Shea, *Starlight*, 127.
[17] Denise Levertov, "Annunciation," quoted in *Starlight*, 124-126.

There is reference here to that moment in today's gospel
when Mary says to the angel Gabriel:
"I am the handmaid of the Lord.
May it be done to me according to your word" (1:38).
She didn't protest, I can't do it.
She didn't say, I'm not worthy.
She didn't submit begrudgingly
or resign herself with a grim reluctance.
"Consent illumined her," and in that way
she did not obscure God's light in her being.

And that's what Mary can teach us to do:
to consent to God's will
with a confident love that will illumine our being,
to do God's will, understanding it
not as some predetermined set of events
to which we must submit,
but as an ongoing expression of God's love
revealed to us through time and circumstance.

That takes great faith and courage,
and Mary had both.
That's why we stand with her now,
just a few days before Christmas,
and ask God to bless us through her,
to let his face shine upon us,
in the person of Jesus Christ his Son.

DECEMBER 21st

Zp 3:14-18;   Lk 1:39-45

MARY'S JOY

We're four days away from Christmas,
and today's readings attempt to fuel our spirits with joy.
"Shout for joy," the prophet Zephaniah says
to the exiles returned to Jerusalem.
"Sing joyfully, O Israel!"
The Lord, your God, is in your midst,
a mighty savior" (3:14, 17).
And in the gospel Elizabeth shouts with joy
when her cousin Mary enters the house and greets her.
Why? Because when Elizabeth heard Mary's greeting,
the child in her womb, she says, leapt with joy.

Mary had traveled in haste from Nazareth in Galilee
to a town in Judah in the hill country.
They say that would take at least four days.
Did she go alone?
That's what Luke seems to say,
but if women in those days went anywhere alone,
they'd be subject to charges of shameful conduct.
"They either had to be always in a cluster of women...
or under the watchful eye of their father...
or some other responsible male relative."
Especially "a fourteen-year-old unmarried girl
like Mary."[18]

---

[18] John J. Pilch, *the Cultural World of Jesus*, 10.

Something that Pope John Paul said
in his reflections on the Visitation
provides us, I think, with a possible explanation.[19]
"In describing Mary's departure for Judea,
the Evangelist uses the verb 'anistemi,'
which means 'to arise,' 'to start moving.'
Considering that this verb is used in the Gospels
to indicate Jesus' Resurrection (Mk 8:31; Lk 24:7, 46)
or physical actions that imply a spiritual effort (Lk 5:27-
28; 15:18, 20), we can suppose that Luke wishes to stress
with this expression the vigorous zeal which led Mary,
under the inspiration of the Holy Spirit,
to give the world its Savior.
Meeting with Elizabeth," he concludes,
"is a joyous event."

And Elizabeth with joy cries out in a loud voice
"Blessed are you among women
and blessed is the fruit of your womb."
Why in Elizabeth's view is Mary
"blessed among women"?
Because she believed.
"Blessed are you," Elizabeth says, "who believed
that what was spoken to you by the Lord
would be fulfilled" (1:45).

Mary's joy arises from that fact.
And we rejoice with her
every time we say the "Hail, Mary."

---

[19] General Audience of October 2, 1996, in Rome.

DECEMBER 22nd
1 S 1:24-28;   Lk 1:46-56

SADNESS AND JOY

In Saul Bellow's novel *Seize the Day*
one character says to another:
"I want to tell you, don't marry [sadness].
Some people do.
They get married to it, and sleep and eat together,
just as husband and wife.
If they go with joy, they think it's adultery."

It's as if sadness, not joy,
were more in tune with the human spirit.
Physiologically, the opposite is true:
sadness constricts blood vessels; joy expands them.

There is an old saying that sorrow shared is halved
and joy shared is doubled.
In one of his last sonnets[20] the Jesuit poet
Gerard Manley Hopkins reminds himself
to "leave comfort root-room; let joy size
At God knows when to God knows what."

Elizabeth says to Mary: "[A]t the moment
the sound of your greeting reached my ears,
the infant in my womb leaped for joy" (Lk 1:44).
And Mary herself declares:
"My spirit rejoices in God my savior."

---

[20] "My own heart let me more have pity on."

Why? Because "he has looked upon my lowliness"
and "has done great things for me" (Lk 1:47-49).
She is to be the mother of the Christ child.

So it was with Hannah.
She prayed and the Lord looked on her with favor.
She conceived and bore Samuel.
"I prayed for this child," we heard her say,
"and the Lord granted my request.
Now I, in turn, give him to the Lord" (1 S 1:28).

And Mary, too, shall give her Son to God,
in much the same spirit as in the prayer
that St. Ignatius has us say in the
Contemplation to Attain Love:
"You have given all to me, now I return it.
All of it is yours.
Dispose of it according to your will."[21]
But Mary's Son will be crucified.
Yes, Jesus will be crucified.
Even as we recognize that fact,
we hear him say at the Last Supper:
"If you loved me, you would rejoice
that I am going to the Father" (Jn 14:28).

---

[21] *The Spiritual Exercises of St. Ignatius*, #234.

DECEMBER 23rd
Ml 3:1-4, 23-24; Lk 1:57-66

PREPARE THE WAY OF THE LORD

Malachi was said to be the last of the prophets.
But five centuries later John the Baptist is born.
Malachi himself declared, as we heard today,
that another prophet would come.
The Lord says:
"Lo, I am sending my messenger
to prepare the way before me…
Lo, I will send you Elijah, the prophet…" (3:1, 23).
Elijah is the prophet who defends Yahweh
as the one and only God
and repudiates the cults of any other god.
He was believed to have been taken up in a fiery chariot
and was expected to return at the end of time.
This hope was very much alive in Jesus' time;
in the minds of some *he* was even thought to be Elijah,
but as Jesus himself declared, *John* is Elijah,
"if you are willing to accept it" (Mt 11:14).

"What will this child be?" (Lk 1:66)
A question posed by the people
who came to celebrate John's remarkable birth.
Malachi provides us with an answer.
He will be the messenger
who prepares the way of the Lord.
And how will he do that?
By turning "the hearts of fathers to their children,
and the hearts of children to their fathers" (3:24).
In other words, he will become for many

an instrument of peace and reconciliation,
and thus prepare the way for the Great Reconciler.

That indicates how we are to prepare for his coming.
Be reconciled — with ourselves, with others,
with our God.

O come, O come, Emmanuel,
King and Judge, Desire of all the nations,
come and set us free, O Lord our God.

DECEMBER 24th
2 S 7:1-5, 8-11, 16;   Lk 1:67-79

THE LIGHT OF CHRIST

When he wrote down that his son was to be named John,
Zechariah's tongue was freed
and he proclaimed the great canticle
known by its first word in Latin, the Benedictus:
"Blessed be the Lord the God of Israel" (1:67).

The canticle is full of praise and prophecy.
Zechariah sees in John's birth
the fulfillment of all the promises made to Israel.
The promise of the covenant to Abraham:
"[the Lord] is mindful of his holy covenant
and of the oath he swore to Abraham our father" (1:73).
The promise of Nathan to David:
"[The Lord] has raised up a horn for our salvation
within the house of David his servant" (1:69).

As we heard Nathan say to David in the first reading:
"Your house and your kingdom
shall endure forever before me;
your throne shall stand firm forever" (2 S 7:16).

All this will be fulfilled in Jesus.
And John, "prophet of the Most High,"
as Zechariah proclaims,
"will go before the Lord to prepare his ways."
What would our world, our life, be like
without the light of Christ, "the daybreak from on high"?
We would be left sitting
"in darkness and death's shadow."

May the light of Christ fill our lives
and shine through us into the lives of others
and "guide our feet into the path of peace" (Lk 1:76-79).

CHRISTMAS SEASON

DECEMBER 26th
St. Stephen, First Martyr
Ac 6:8-10; 7:54-59;   Mt 10:17-22

REJOICING AND MOURNING

Why do we celebrate St. Stephen's feast day
immediately after Christmas?
One answer is because historically the Church
was probably observing his feast day
on the 26th before December 25th was fixed
as the day of Christ's birth.[22]
Maybe so. But if so,
why wasn't it changed to another date?
After all, there's no reason to believe that December 26th
was actually the day of St. Stephen's martyrdom.

I think Archbishop Thomas Becket
in T.S. Eliot's *Murder in the Cathedral*
supplies us with a very good answer.
The archbishop is preaching in the cathedral
on Christmas morning.
"Dear children of God....
Is it an accident, do you think,
that the day of the first martyr
follows immediately the day of the Birth of Christ?
By no means. Just as we rejoice and mourn at once,
in the Birth and in the Passion of Our Lord;
so also, in a smaller figure,
we both rejoice and mourn in the death of martyrs.

---

[22] *The Vatican II Weekday Missal,* 167.

We mourn,
for the sins of the world that has martyred them;
we rejoice,
that another soul is numbered
among the Saints in Heaven,
for the glory of God and for the salvation of men."[23]

In contemplating the Nativity in the Spiritual Exercises,
we're told to consider what Mary and Joseph "are doing,
for example, journeying and toiling,
in order that the Lord may be born in greatest poverty;
and after so many hardships of hunger, thirst,
heat, and cold, injuries, and insults,
he may die on the cross! And all this for me!"[24]

Rejoicing and mourning
are implicit in the very name of Jesus.
Jesus means "God saves."
How does God save?
By Christ's birth, yes.
But ultimately by his passion and death.
And then his resurrection.

Rejoice and mourn, St. Thomas Becket says.
The one doesn't cancel out the other.
The one doesn't dilute the other.
But in this connection I remember that old saying:
Sorrow shared is halved and joy shared is doubled.

---

[23] *Murder in the Cathedral*, Interlude.

[24] *The Spiritual Exercises of Saint Ignatius*, #116 (Ganss trans.)

DECEMBER 27th
St. John, Apostle and Evangelist
1 Jn 1:1-4; Jn 20:2-8

THE FIRSTBORN

John the apostle is also an evangelist.
Matthew, Mark, Luke, and John —
of these four he is the only one
who refers to Jesus as the "Word."[25]
"In the beginning was the Word,
and the Word was with God,
and the Word was God" (Jn 1:1).
That opens the prologue of his gospel,
and we heard an echo of it today
in the prologue of his first letter:
"What was from the beginning,
what we have heard,
what we have seen with our eyes,
what we looked upon
and touched with our hands
concerns the Word of life" (1 Jn 1:1).

John proclaims to us what he has seen and heard
so that we might share fellowship with him —
fellowship "with the Father
and with his son Jesus Christ" (1 Jn 1:3).

But in the gospel there is no seeing or touching.
To have seen Jesus' body —
that is, to have seen his corpse —

---

[25] Tylenda, *Saints of the Liturgical Year*, 176.

when he went with Simon Peter to the tomb
would have meant not the beginning but the end.
But John did see something.
He saw the burial cloths,
and the cloth that had covered Jesus' head,
"not with the burial cloths
but rolled up in a separate place" (20:7).
John "saw and believed" (20:9).

The same Jesus who was with the Father
and became visible to us
is now with the Father in glory.
And he is now with us through the Spirit.
He, the firstborn, is born in us through the Spirit.
We are, as it were, incarnations of the Word of life;
we are, as Jesus is, and as he said of us,
"the light of the world" (Mt 5:14).

John's purpose in writing all this
is to fill us with joy.
Like the angel, he gives us tidings of great joy
to be shared with all the people (Lk 2:10).

DECEMBER 28th
Holy Innocents, Martyrs
1 Jn 1:5-2:2;   Mt 2:13-18

CROWNED WITH LIFE

As we heard in the first reading, "God is light,
and there is no darkness in him at all" (1 Jn 1:5).
There is no darkness in him at all;

darkness is not in God but in the world.
"The light shines in the darkness," John says,
and the darkness has not overcome it" (Jn 1:5).

The darkness that has not overcome the light
is nonetheless a powerful threat to the newborn child.
The child's appearance actually provokes the darkness.
Herod is determined to kill him
and, lacking precise information,
he orders "the massacre of all the boys in Bethlehem
and its vicinity two years old and under" (Mt 2:16).
Of course, even without Herod,
over half the children born in Jesus' time
would die before the age of two.

In this account of the massacre of the holy innocents
we have an echo of the Old Testament story of Moses.
In order to stop the growth of the Israelites in Egypt,
the Pharaoh ordered that every boy be killed (Ex 1:22).
But the baby Moses is rescued by Pharaoh's daughter
and he becomes the savior of his people.

The Jewish historian Josephus does not record
the slaughter of the innocents in Jesus' time,
but he does make mention of Herod's barbarity.
Because Bethlehem was a small town,
the number of male children killed
was probably somewhere between twenty or thirty.

With their death and the death of every innocent in mind,
consider now what we will pray after Communion:
"Lord, by a wordless profession of faith in your Son,
the innocents were crowned with life at his birth.
May all people who receive your holy gifts today
come to share in the fullness of salvation."

DECEMBER 29th
Fifth Day in the Octave of Christmas
1 Jn 2:3-11; Lk 2:22-35

RECOGNITION

Recognition is an important element in drama.
Aristotle in his *Poetics*
says that the best kind of recognition
is the recognition of who a person is or was or will be.
And drama after all is an imitation of life.

As we heard in today's gospel,
"It had been revealed" to Simeon "by the Holy Spirit"
that he would not see death
"before he had seen the Messiah,"
the Christ, the Anointed of the Lord (Lk 2:26).
Mary and Joseph bring the child Jesus into the temple,
and as soon as Simeon sees him
he recognizes him for what he is,
and takes him into his arms and blesses God, saying:
"…my eyes have seen your salvation,
which you prepared in sight of all the peoples,
a light for revelation to the Gentiles,
and glory for your people Israel" (2:30-32).

With the eyes of faith
we too recognize him for what he is.

In the first reading John suggests
that recognition is affirmed by action.
"The way we may be sure," he says,
"that we know [Jesus] is to keep his commandments.
Whoever says, 'I know him,'

but does not keep his commandments is a liar,
and the truth is not in him" (1 Jn 2:3-4).

Here and now, guided by the Holy Spirit,
let us recognize him in the breaking of the bread.

DECEMBER 30th
Sixth Day in the Octave of Christmas
1 Jn 2:12-17;   Lk 2:36-40

SIDE BY SIDE BEFORE GOD

Anna — the name means "grace, favor."
It's the Greek form of the Hebrew Hannah.
Hannah was the name of Samuel's mother.
And Anna, of course, was the name of Mary's mother.

Anna the prophetess, whom we met in today's gospel,
recognizes the child Jesus as the one who is to come.
Like Simeon, she gives thanks to God
and speaks about the child to everybody
there in the temple longing for redemption.

The pairing of Simeon and Anna foreshadows
an impressive theme in Luke:
the theme of "man and woman [standing] together
and side by side before God.
They are equal in honour and grace,
they are endowed with the same gifts
and have the same responsibilities."[26]

---

[26] H. Flender, *St. Luke*, quoted in *The New Jerome Biblical Commentary*, 684.

Other pairings, to name just a few, include
the centurion and the widow of Naim (7:1-17),
Simon the Pharisee and the sinful woman (7:36-50),
the women at the tomb and the disciples
on the way to Emmaus (23:55-24:35).

Anna, we're told, "never left the temple,
but worshiped night and day
with fasting and prayer" (2:37).

If we join with her in spirit,
we will recognize the meaning of the entrance Antiphon:
"When peaceful silence lay over all,
and night had run half of her swift course,
your all-powerful word, O Lord,
leaped down from heaven,
from the royal throne" (Ws 18:14-15).

DECEMBER 31st
Seventh Day in the Octave of Christmas
1 Jn 2:18-21;   Jn 1:1-18

THE LAST HOUR

"Children," John says, this is "the last hour" (1 Jn 2:18).
For John, the last hour is the end of time.
For us, hearing it read on the seventh day
in the Octave of Christmas, it is the last hour of the year.

The great truths of Christmas are reiterated.
John, in the first reading, says,

"you have the anointing
that comes from the holy one,
and you all have knowledge" (1 Jn 2:20).
The "holy one" most likely refers to Christ,
to *Christos*, the Anointed One.
If we have the anointing that comes from him,
we have become others Christs.
We have been born into the truth, the revelation of God,
into the mystery of God revealed in Jesus.

The gospel is a powerful expression of this truth.
"In the beginning was the Word...
and the Word became flesh
and made his dwelling among us,
and we have seen his glory:
the glory of an only Son coming from the Father,
full of grace and truth" (Jn 1:1, 14).
Full of grace and truth, that is to say,
Jesus is the fullness of God's gift,
which *is* the truth, the revelation of God in time.
"From his fullness we have all received,
grace in the place of grace" (2:16),
the new in place of the old.
For while the law was a gift through Moses,
grace and truth came through Jesus Christ.
Christ here is the gift "and the revelation
which replaces the law." And we, the children of God,
"share in the 'fullness' of Jesus, the Word made flesh,"
the firstborn of all creation.[27]

With this in mind, we pray again as we prayed
in the opening prayer: "Ever-living God...

---

[27] James McPolin, S.J., *John*, 39.

help us to share in the life of Christ
for he is the salvation of all mankind."
And then, as we shall pray in the prayer over the gifts,
"[B]y our sharing in this mystery
draw us closer to each other and to you."

JANUARY 2nd (before Epiphany)
Sts. Basil the Great and Gregory Nazianzen
1 Jn 2:22-28; Jn 1:19-28

OTHER CHRISTS

Who is the Messiah, who is the Christ?
That question comes up in both readings
and in the lives of today's saints,
Basil the Great and Gregory Nazianzen.
In the gospel we're told that priests and Levites
were sent from Jerusalem to ask John the Baptist
a very important question: "Who are you?"
"I am not the Messiah," he says, "I am not the Christ.
I am the voice of the one who cries out in the desert,
'Make straight the way of the Lord'" (Jn 1:22-23).
And the Lord, he implies, has already come;
the Messiah, the Christ, is already in their midst:
"there is one among you whom you do not recognize…
whose sandal strap I am not worthy to untie" (1:26-27).

In the first reading, from a letter of John the apostle
addressed to a Christian community, we learn
that even among Christians there were some
who did not recognize Jesus for what he is.

"Who is the liar?" John asks, and this is his answer:
"Whoever denies that Jesus is the Christ" (1 Jn 2:22).
Whoever denies him is, of course, an Antichrist.
"Let what you heard from the beginning remain in you.
If what you heard from the beginning remains in you,
then you will remain in the Son and in the Father" (2:24).
You will, in effect, be other Christs.

Saints Basil and Gregory were great friends.
The big heresy in their day, in the fourth century,
was Arianism, according to which,
Christ was not truly human,
but was rather a divine being encased in flesh.
And yet neither was he *fully* divine,
because he was not equal to the Father.
Basil and Gregory, of course, proclaimed Christ
to be true God and true man,
and this belief suffused their whole lives.

Gregory, writing of his friendship with Basil, says:
"Different men have different names,
which they owe to their parents or to themselves,
that is, to their own pursuits and achievements.
But our great pursuit, the great name we wanted,
was to be Christians, to be called Christians."[28]

To be Christians, to be other Christs:
that is our great pursuit, too.
As John said, let what you heard from the beginning
remain in your hearts.

---

[28] *The Liturgy of the Hours*, I, 1287.

JANUARY 3rd (before Epiphany)
1 Jn 2:29-3:6;   Jn 1:29-34

THE LAMB OF GOD

There is a clear link between the two readings:
In the first reading John the evangelist says:
"You know that [God's Son] was revealed
to take away sins, and in him there is no sin" (1 Jn 3:5).
And in the gospel John the Baptist says:
"[T]he reason why I came baptizing with water
was that he might be made known to Israel" (Jn 1:31).
And when he sees Jesus coming:
"Behold, the Lamb of God,
who takes away the sin of the world!" (1:30).

In other words, Jesus is coming to do
what his name declares: God saves,
that is, God takes away the sin of the world.
How? By Jesus' passion and death
and his rising to new life in the Spirit.
This is what John the Baptist implies
when he calls him the Lamb of God.

That title is rich with allusions.
There is one that I came across recently
which I hadn't adverted to before.[29]
In the story of Abraham's intended sacrifice of Isaac
there is a prophecy not fulfilled in the story.
The child Isaac asks his father Abraham,
"Where is the lamb for the whole-burnt offering?"

---

[29] Cf. Stanley, "I Encountered God!", 77.

Abraham answers: "God himself will provide a lamb
as whole-burnt offering, my son."
But after the climax of the story,
it's not a lamb, but a ram, that is provided.
John the evangelist,
recording the words of John the Baptist,
apparently found Abraham's prophecy
fulfilled in Jesus' atoning death:
Jesus is the lamb that God provides.
Jesus, as John the Baptist says, is God's chosen One.

And when Jesus saves us, taking away our sins,
he makes us like himself — for "in him there is no sin" —
he makes us God's children.
"See what love the Father has bestowed on us
that we may be called the children of God" (1 Jn 3:1).
As children of God
we are filled with trust and confidence.
As children of God
we are sure of God's guidance and forgiveness.
As children of God
we live in the light of his love.

JANUARY 4th (before Epiphany)
St. Elizabeth Ann Seton, Religious
1 Jn 3:7-10; Jn 1:35-42

A GREAT JOY

Andrew appears three times in John's gospel,
each time introducing somebody to Jesus.
In today's gospel he introduces his brother Simon.

Jesus looks at him and says to him right off:
"'[Y]ou will be called Kephas [the Rock],'
(which is translated Peter)" (Jn 1:42).
In the second incident Andrew brings to Jesus
the boy with the five loaves and two fishes (Jn 6:9).
The third incident occurs when some Greeks
who had come to Jerusalem for the Passover
tell Andrew that they would like to see Jesus
and Andrew brings them to him (Jn 12:20-22).
"It was Andrew's great joy to bring others to Jesus."[30]

Elizabeth Ann Seton, a believing Episcopalian,
was introduced to Jesus at a deeper level
by a Catholic family in Italy,
where she had gone for her husband's health.
When her husband died,
Elizabeth Ann returned to New York,
and she was received into the Church.
Later, she founded the Sisters of Charity,
and as their number grew,
so did their schools and orphanages,[31]
where many children were introduced to Jesus.
This was her joy, to introduce others to Jesus.

May it also be ours.

---

[30] Barclay, *The Gospel of John*, vol.1, 89.
[31] Tylenda, *Saints of the Liturgical Year*, 2.

JANUARY 5th (before Epiphany)
St. John Neumann, Bishop
1 Jn 3:11-21; Jn 1:43-51

THE LADDER BETWEEN HEAVEN AND EARTH

Yesterday Andrew sought out his brother Simon Peter
and introduced him to Jesus.
Today Philip seeks out Nathanael.
In doing this Andrew is following the pattern
of the first disciples in John's gospel:
One disciple introducing another to Jesus.
The vocation of a disciple, of a missionary, is this:
to receive and share the good news,
and the good news is Jesus Christ himself.

John Neumann, whose memory we celebrate today,
"is the first U.S. bishop to be canonized a saint."[32]
He was born in Bohemia (now the Czech Republic).
While studying in Prague,
he decided to be a missionary in the United States.
Ordained a priest in New York City,
he worked for a time in Buffalo,
then entered the Redemptorist Order
and served as a parish priest in Pittsburgh and Baltimore.
Pope Pius IX appointed him fourth bishop of Philadelphia.
"During his eight years as bishop he built eighty churches
and organized Philadelphia's diocesan school system."
He spoke English with a heavy German accent
and at first he was not all that well received,
but soon the light of Christ shone through,

---

[32] Tylenda, *Saints of the Liturgical Year*, 3.

and the people knew that they had a saint in their midst,
which is to say, he brought the good news,
he brought Jesus himself, into their lives.

Nathanael believed because Jesus saw him
under the fig tree, because Jesus saw into his heart.
"You will see greater things than this," Jesus said (1:50).
Nathanael will see greater things in Jesus himself:
the Word made flesh, splendor of the Father,
the ladder between heaven and earth.

January 6th (before Epiphany)

1 Jn 5:5-13;   Mk 1:7-11

GRATITUDE

I think of the refrain of a simple English hymn:
"Thou, that hast given so much to me,
give me one thing more: a grateful heart."
Gratitude — *eucharistia* in Greek —
is a gift of the Holy Spirit.
It is, in fact, the Holy Spirit,
"the Spirit of truth" (1 Jn 5:6),
who testifies to all the good things God has to give.
God gives the Holy Spirit in all good things
and gives all good things in the Holy Spirit.
I say this because I think Jesus said as much,
or would have us so understand him.
Once, speaking of prayer, he said to his disciples:
"Which one of you would hand his son a stone
when he asks for a loaf of bread?...

If you, then, who are wicked,
know how to give good gifts to your children,
how much more will your heavenly Father
give good things to those who ask him?" (Mt 7:9-11).
Luke reports this saying with an interesting variation:
Instead of saying "give good things" he has Jesus say:
"give the Holy Spirit to those who ask him?" (11:13).

In asking for the Holy Spirit
we are asking for all that is good;
in asking for whatever is good
we are asking for the Holy Spirit.
God gives us his Spirit in Jesus Christ,
"from whom all good things come,"
as we say in the Eucharistic Prayer III.

The baptism of Jesus reported in today's gospel
somehow captures all this in a single image:
"On coming up out of the water
[John] saw the heavens being torn open
and the Spirit, like a dove, descending upon him.
And a voice came from the heavens,
'You are my beloved Son;
with you I am well pleased'" (Mk 1:10-11).
The Holy Spirit enables us, as it enabled John,
to recognize Jesus as the beloved of God,
as one whom God sends in the fullness of time
"so that we might receive adoption," as St. Paul says.
As proof that we are God's children,
"God [sends] the Spirit of his Son into our hearts
crying out, 'Abba, Father!'" (Gal 4:5-6);
and "if children, then heirs, heirs of God
and joint heirs with Christ" (Rm 8:17).
Having given us his own Son, Paul continues,

"how will [God] not also give us
everything else along with him?" (Rm 8:32).

All this is made manifest to us
in that shining moment when Jesus comes up
out of the waters of his baptism.
Here, surely, is a cause for supreme gratitude,
for letting the Holy Spirit well up in our hearts
and bear witness to all the good things
God has to give in Christ.
"Thou, that has given so much to me,
give one thing more: a grateful heart."

With grateful hearts, therefore, pray God
that we may always cherish his gifts
and see them multiply even as we share them.[33]

January 7th (before Epiphany)
1 Jn 5:14-21;   Jn 2:1-12

THE GIFT OF GOD

At the wedding at Cana,
Jesus performs the first of his signs,
the first of his miracles meant to reveal
the power and glory of God.
"Do whatever he tells you,"
Mary says to the servers (Jn 2:5).

---

[33] Adapted from *The Paths of Life, Cycle B*, 33-35.

And Jesus changes water into wine.
Thus he "revealed his glory" (2:11).
In Hebrew thought, "glory" is the presence of God.
In Jesus, the presence of God is made manifest.
This is what the disciples saw,
this is why they "began to believe in him" (2:11).

Who is this Jesus?
In the way John tells the story
he guides us to an answer of sorts.
Note that no mention is made in this story
of the bride and bridegroom as such. Why?
Because, for John, Jesus is the bridegroom.
In the very next chapter he has John the Baptist say:
"The one who has the bride is the bridegroom;
the best man, who stands and listens for him,
rejoices greatly at the bridegroom's voice.
So this joy of mine has been made complete" (3:29).
This same John had leapt for joy in his mother's womb
when Mary, still pregnant with Jesus, visited her;
now he says his joy is complete
because Jesus the bridegroom is at hand.
Isaiah's words are fulfilled in Jesus:
"[Y]ou shall be called 'My Delight.'
As a bridegroom rejoices in his bride,
so shall your God rejoice in you" (62:4-5).

This, too, the disciples "saw" or perceived;
for this reason, too, they believed in Jesus.
God had revealed himself before in diverse ways;
now, in the changing of water into wine,
God reveals his glory, his presence,
a loving and potent presence, in Christ Jesus.
We, too, are called to believe in him.

"Whoever is begotten by God," says St. John,
"conquers the world." How? By "our faith" (1 Jn 5:4).
The world, of itself, would consume us
with its greed, its lust, its violence,
its deceit, its meaninglessness.

But we by our faith must conquer it,
that is, refuse to be taken in by its values,
refuse to let ourselves be deceived;
instead, we give meaning to our lives
by our faith in Christ Jesus,
who rescues us from meaninglessness.
We are meant to be like the gulf stream,
in the ocean and yet distinct from it,
warming the globe as it courses around the world,
a gift to the globe of this world.
Without it life would freeze over.

Jesus, a gift to us and our gift to others,
a gift given from the heart of Mary in time,
a sign of giving from the heart of God from all eternity;
a gift, yes, but also a demand, an urgency, a challenge:
we are urged, challenged, to believe in him,
to be what he is, to do what he does,
that the world may be filled with his joy.[34]

---

[34] Adapted from *The Paths of Life, Cycle C*, 105-107.

MONDAY (after Epiphany)
1 Jn 3:22-4:6;   Mt 4:12-17, 23-25

WHAT WILL THIS CHILD BE?

What will this child be?
That was the question asked about
Elizabeth and Zechariah's baby John:
But with even greater wonder
it is asked implicitly of the baby Jesus:
What will this child be?
In the gospel for the feast of the Epiphany,
we heard this answer:
From you, Bethlehem, "shall come a ruler
who is to shepherd my people Israel" (Mt 2:6).
And not just the people of Israel:
he is to shepherd all people,
represented by the three wise men
who come and do him homage.

Today's gospel shows this answer unfolding in the future.
Jesus, already advanced in age and grace and wisdom,
now begins announcing God's kingdom,
not just to the Jews but to the Gentiles as well.
He leaves Nazareth
and goes to live in Capernaum by the sea,
in the region of Zebulun and Naphtali,
the "Galilee of the Gentiles,"
to fulfill what had been said by the prophet Isaiah:
"'the people who sit in darkness have seen a great light;
on those dwelling in a land overshadowed by death
light has arisen'" (Mt 4:15-16).
Jesus went about proclaiming

the good news of the kingdom,
and curing the people of every illness.
And great crowds followed him,
not just from Judea but from the Ten Cities as well,
not just Jews therefore, but Gentiles as well.

This becomes the mission of every disciple, then and now,
to proclaim the good news to all the people.
The fruit of any missionary's labor
is fidelity to God's commandment.
As the apostle John expresses it in today's first reading,
God's "commandment is this:
we should believe in the name of his Son, Jesus Christ,
and love one another just as he commanded us" (3:23).

May that fruit ripen in our lives:
to believe in Jesus, born of woman,
sent to us by God his Father
because God so loved the world,
and to love one another just as he commanded us.

TUESDAY (after Epiphany)
1 Jn 4:7-10;   Mk 6:34-44

BE LIKE GOD

Bill and Kathy Magee are a married couple
who live very much in the spirit of today's gospel.
Bill, a plastic surgeon, and Kathy, a registered nurse,
have created a service called Operation Smile.
In this country and in countries around the world

they correct birth defects and deformities in children,
reaching out to about 4,000 children a year.
"We were both raised in Catholic families," Kathy says,
"and Bill was mostly in Jesuit schools.
That whole Jesuit philosophy is 'men for others,'
that you should really 'give back' at some point.
I think we got that spirit from our backgrounds."[35]

In the gospel Jesus sees "the vast crowd"
and his heart is "moved with pity for them" (Mk 6:34).
When his disciples tell him to dismiss them
so that they can go get something to eat,
Jesus says in reply:
"Give them some food yourselves" (6:37).
Share what you have. Thank God for it.
Give it away. Give it to the hungry. Let it multiply.
Jesus is saying, in effect, "that the whole point
of anyone's life is to nourish others."[36]

In other words, be like God.
In the first reading, God showed his love for us
by sending "his only Son into the world
so that we might have life through him" (1 Jn 4:9).
Inspired by that love,
Jesus shared his very life with us,
an action that we celebrate here and now
in the Eucharist, the bread of life.

---

[35] *Biography*, January 1997, 24-28.
[36] Frank Andersen, M.S.C., *Imagine Jesus...*, 57.

WEDNESDAY (after Epiphany)
1 Jn 4:11-18;   Mk 6:45-52

REVELATION

The image of Jesus walking on water
is an image of singular power.
After feeding the five thousand,
Jesus had made his disciples
leave in their boats without him.
And now, in "the fourth watch of the night"
(about three hours before dawn),
they are caught in the middle of the lake,
struggling against the wind.
Suddenly they see him.
"It is a ghost!" they say.
And they cry out in fear.
But immediately Jesus speaks to them,
"Take courage, it is I; do not be afraid!" (Mk 6:50).
He comes to them, walking on the sea,
seeming almost to rise out of it.
He comes to them like a pillar of light
cleaving the darkness,
and the waves bow down before him.

The image is radiant with divinity.
Jesus intends "to pass by them" (6:48).
Although the words mean literally what they say,
when said of God in the Old Testament (1 K 19:11)
and of Jesus here and elsewhere in the gospels (Mt 20:30),
they connote epiphany:
"to pass by" is "to manifest oneself."
A striking parallel occurs in the Book of Job:

the God who "trampled the waves of the sea" (9:8)
"passes by" Job, but Job sees him not (9:11).[37]

The words that Jesus speaks
bring to the image an even greater power.
"Take courage, it is I, do not be afraid!"
Expressions such as these are often used
in a theophanic context,
as when the Lord reveals himself to Abram (Gn 15:1).
Jesus not only identifies himself;
he also reveals himself,
using what is called the "revelation formula":
"It is I" (literally, "I am"),
the name revealed to Moses
from the heart of the burning bush (Ex 3:14).
After the disciples had left him,
Jesus had gone off by himself to pray;
and now, still in communion with his Father,
he speaks out of the depths of his being:
"Take courage. It is I. Do not be afraid!"

As we heard in the first reading:
"There is no fear in love...
perfect love drives out fear" (1 Jn 4:18).

---

[37] Cf. *The Jerome Biblical Commentary*, vol. 2, 36.

THURSDAY (after Epiphany)
1 Jn 4:19-5:4;   Lk 4:14-22

THE GIFT OF THE SPIRIT

We've celebrated the feast of the Epiphany,
but we're still very much in the season of Epiphany.
The gospel today is a leap to the beginning
of Christ's public ministry;
it can also be seen as an epiphany
that Jesus himself makes of himself.
Reading from the prophet Isaiah, he declares:
"The Spirit of the Lord is upon me";
the Spirit "has anointed me" (Lk 4:18),
that is, has made me Christ, the Messiah.
An earlier text from Isaiah
concerning the Spirit and Christ the Messiah, reads:
"[A] shoot shall sprout from the stump of Jesse,
and from his roots a bud shall blossom.
The spirit of the Lord shall rest upon him:
A spirit of wisdom and understanding...
of counsel and of strength... of knowledge...
and of fear of the Lord" (Is 11:1-3).

Pope John Paul II in his encyclical
on the Holy Spirit in the Church and the World
calls this a bridge text
between the ancient biblical concept
understood as "charismatic breath or wind,"
and spirit as a person and a gift.
Clearly such is the Spirit for Christ in today's gospel:
"The Spirit of the Lord is upon me,
because he has anointed me

to bring glad tidings to the poor.
He has sent me to proclaim liberty to captives
and recovery of sight to the blind,
to let the oppressed go free,
and to proclaim a year acceptable to the Lord" (4:18-19).
And then Jesus declares: "Today this scripture passage
is fulfilled in your hearing" (4:21).
Jesus is given the gift of the Spirit
and now Jesus the Christ brings
the gifts of the Spirit to others.

In the first reading, John says:
"Everyone who believes Jesus is the Christ
is begotten of God" (1 Jn 5:1). And later:
"[W]hoever is begotten by God conquers the world.
And the victory that conquers the world
is our faith" (5:4).
Faith, as John understands it, is linked to love.
Faith is to believe that Jesus is the Christ,
the one anointed by the Spirit, the one sent;
faith is to believe that God so loved the world
that he sent his only Son to be our Christ and Savior.
If God so loved the world, the men and women in it,
how can we not love them, our brothers and sisters,
if we say we love God?

FRIDAY (after Epiphany)

1 Jn 5:5-13; Lk 5:12-16

THE THEME OF FAITH

John's first letter is like a musical composition.
It develops themes with variations.
The theme in today's reading is the theme of faith.
"Believe" God, John says (5:10). Accept God's word.
God is not a liar!
"Believe in" God's testimony concerning his Son (5:11):
God gives us eternal life and this life is in his Son.
"Believe that" what God reveals is true (5:5):
Jesus is the Son of God.[38]

The theme of faith is also heard in the gospel.
A man "full of leprosy" comes to Jesus.
A man full of faith:
"Lord, if you wish, you can make me clean" (Lk 5:12).
This is an occasion of yet another epiphany,
the epiphany of Jesus the healer; an occasion
of another manifestation of his power and love:
"I do will it. Be made clean" (5:13).
The Word made flesh touches untouchable flesh
and brings it to life again.

But that is not the end of it.
It is a sign of what is to come.
Jesus came that we might have life — eternal life.
As we heard John say: "God gave us eternal life,
and this life is in his Son" (1 Jn 5:11).

---

[38] Cf. *Revelation and the General Epistles*, 120.

And in the verse immediately following today's reading,
he says: "I write these things to you
so that you may know that you have eternal life,
you who believe in the name of the Son of God" (5:13).

As we prayed in the opening prayer:
"May he continue to guide us with his light."

SATURDAY (after Epiphany)
1 Jn 5:14-21; Jn 3:22-30

ANOTHER EPIPHANY

Hardly a day goes by that we don't disagree
with someone about something,
some opinion, some decision, some way of proceeding,
something we see, something we hear, something we read,
sometimes very minor, sometimes not so minor.
It's very much a part of being human.

In today's readings,
both John the Baptist and the Apostle John
have to deal with disagreements among their disciples,
disagreements over Jesus.
Earlier in his letter John mentions persons
who have separated themselves from the community
because of their failure to accept the truth about Jesus.
He calls them dissidents and "antichrists" (1 Jn 2:18).
When in today's reading he speaks of those
whose sin is "deadly" or mortal (5:16),
it is thought that he has reference to these dissidents.

"We… know," he says, "that the Son of God
has come and has given us discernment
to know the one who is true.
And we are in the one who is true,
in his Son Jesus Christ" (5:20).

In the gospel, John the Baptist is met by his disciples
who are very much put out
by all the attention that Jesus is getting.
"[H]ere he is baptizing," they say,
"And everyone is coming to him" (Jn 3:26).
In the very next chapter, by the way,
it is stated that Jesus himself did not baptize,
only his disciples did.
John answers: "You yourselves can testify
that I said [that] I am not the Messiah,
but that I was sent before him."
And he compares himself to the bridegroom's best man
who "rejoices greatly at the bridegroom's voice.
So this joy of mine has been made complete.
He must increase; I must decrease" (3:28-30).
John, in effect, announces another epiphany of Jesus
before he himself retires from the scene.

John invites his disciples and he invites us, too,
to rejoice with him in the bridegroom Jesus.
Hopefully we can all agree to do just that,
to rejoice with him in Jesus.

WORKS CITED

Andersen, Frank, M.S.C. *Imagine Jesus...* Liguori, MO: Liguori Publications, 1994.

Barclay, William. *The Gospel of John*, Vol. 1. Philadelphia: The Westminster Press, 1975.

Bellow, Saul. *Seize the Day*. New York: Viking Press, 1961.

Eliot, T.S. *Murder in the Cathedral*. New York: Harcourt, Brace, 1935.

Ferlita, Ernest, S.J. *The Paths of Life, Cycle A, B, C.* Staten Island, NY: Alba House, 1992, 1993, 1994.

_____. *Gospel Journey.* Minneapolis: Winston Press, 1983.

Herbstrith, Waltraud. *Edith Stein*, tr. by Bernard Bonowitz. San Francisco: Harper & Row, 1985.

Hopkins, Gerard Manley. *The Poems and Prose of Gerard Manley Hopkins*, selected and edited by W.H. Gardner. New York: Penguin Books, 1983.

_____. *The Sermons and Devotional Writings of Gerard Manley Hopkins*, ed. by Christopher Devlin, S.J. London: Oxford University Press, 1959.

Link, Mark, S.J. *Advent/Christmas 2000, Year C.* Allen, TX: Thomas More Publishing, 1996.

The Liturgy of the Hours. New York: Catholic Book Publishing Company, 1976.

Loose-Leaf Lectionary for Mass. Collegeville, MN: The Liturgical Press, 1998.

McPolin, James, S.J. *John.* Wilmington, DE: Michael Glazier, 1979.

Meier, John P. *Matthew.* Collegeville, MN: The Liturgical Press, 1990. (Michael Glazier, 1980).

Moore, Brian, S.J. *The Gospel Day by Day through Advent.* Collegeville, MN: The Liturgical Press, 1989.

The New Jerome Biblical Commentary, edited by Raymond E. Brown, S.S., Joseph A. Fitzmyer, S.J., Roland E. Murphy, O.Carm. Englewood Cliffs, NJ: Prentice Hall, 1990.

O'Collins, Gerald, S.J. *All Things New.* New York: Paulist Press, 1998.

Pilch, John J. *The Cultural World of Jesus, Sunday by Sunday, Cycle C.* Collegeville, MN: The Liturgical Press, 1997.

Revelation and the General Epistles, edited by Charles M. Laymon. Nashville, TN: Abingdon Press, 1983.

Shea, John. *Gospel Spirituality: An Audio Retreat.* Chicago: ACTA Publications, 1994.

_____. *Starlight.* New York: Crossroad, 1992.

The Spiritual Exercises of St. Ignatius. A Translation and Commentary by George E. Ganss, S.J. St. Louis: The Institute of Jesuit Sources, 1992.

Stanley, David M., S.J. "I Encountered God!" *The Spiritual Exercises with the Gospel of John.* St. Louis: The Institute of Jesuit Sources, 1986.

Tardiff, Emiliano. *Jesus Is the Messiah.* South Bend, IN: Greenlawn Press, 1992.

Tylenda, Joseph N., S.J. *Saints of the Liturgical Year: Brief Biographies.* Washington, DC: Georgetown University Press, 1989.

The Vatican II Weekday Missal. Boston: The Daughters of St. Paul, 1975.